A STRUGGLE TO PEACE

A STORY OF A SIXTH

GENERATION MORMON

A STRUGGLE TO PEACE

COPYRIGHT © 2003

CREATIVE SERVICES AND PRINTING THROUGH:
CSN BOOKS PUBLISHING
1975 JANICH RANCH COURT
EL CAJON, CA 92019-1150
TOLL FREE: 1-866-484-6184
CSNbooks.com

PRINTED IN THE UNITED STATES OF AMERICA

Contents

I Felt Very Special

Out of all the millions of people in the world, I held it a privilege to be one of those born into a Mormon home. I cherished my Mormon heritage, thinking I was very special to God, because he had placed me into a family who belonged to "the only true church"[1] and I knew this put me ahead of many people in my advancement towards my becoming a goddess along with my husband becoming a god over our own world.[2]

I started attending the LDS church as an infant and received my name and blessing by the hand of my father when I was three months old. The only religious training I had were the teachings of the Church of Jesus Christ of Latter-day Saints.

As a Mormon, I was taught that there were many gods, but **we served the god of this world, whose name is Elohim**.[3] Elohim lived near the planet Kolob.[4] We were taught he was once a mortal man, who through obedience to Mormon laws and ordinances was exalted to the status of godhood,[5] just like his father before him, to eternity past.[6]

Lucifer Wanted to be the Savior

Elohim (the god of Mormonism) is a polygamist.[7] The number of wives he has is unknown. These wives bore to him billions of spiritual babies. These spiritual children lived with him and his wives in a pre-existent realm.

We were taught that the pre-existence was a place where every human being born on earth lived as one of these spirit children.[8] Elohim saw that his children needed to advance farther, so he decided it was time for them to take a physical body upon the earth to undergo the experiences of mortality.

Thus, Elohim called together a council of the gods to decide the destiny of all those who would be sent to earth. **Two of Elohim's sons were there: Jehovah** (the first born and the Mormon Jesus) **and Lucifer**. As Mormons we believed **Jesus and Lucifer were spirit brothers**, as well as spirit brothers to all mankind.[9]

Mormonism teaches that **Lucifer presented his plan to be the savior** of the world. Getting the glory for himself, he would redeem all mankind without allowing one soul to be lost.[10] Jesus said he would give men their free agency of choice as on all other worlds before. **The council of the gods rejected Lucifer's plan and accepted Jesus' plan**. Angered, Lucifer led a rebellion in heaven where he convinced one third of Elohim's spirit children to rebel with him. He became Satan and was cast out. One third of the spirit children who rebelled with him became the demons and were sent to earth where they were denied physical bodies forever.[11]

Mormon theology states that during this war in heaven, all of those spirit children of Elohim who were unfaithful and not valiant **came to earth cursed with black skin**.[12] Those who were more noble were born into Mormon homes.[13] Therefore, I felt it was **my reward from God** to be born in these last days, into a white Mormon home.

I Wanted to be a Mormon Missionary

As a child, I would sit in my primary class and sing the songs, "I Am A Child of God" and "I Hope They Call Me on a Mission," hoping that someday I could fulfill a mission for the Mormon church. I wanted to be a missionary.

At the age of eight, as with almost every Mormon boy or girl, I was baptized by immersion for the remission of sins[14] by my father, who having the "proper authority" held the Melchizedek priesthood. According to Mormonism, only Mormon men have been bestowed with the authority to baptize and marry. Their priesthood consists of two parts; the Aaronic and the Melchizedek.[15] I was then confirmed a member of the Church of Jesus Christ of Latter-day Saints.

Even as a child, I was eager to learn about the Mormon church, which I was told was the only true church upon the face of the earth. **Joseph Smith**, who was the founder and first "prophet" of the LDS church, **at the age of fourteen**, claimed to have wanted to know what denomination he should join, (having heard of Methodist, Presbyterian and Baptist faiths). He went into the woods to pray. There **he said he had a vision** in which two personages he claimed was God the Father and Jesus Christ appeared to him and told him he must join none of the **Christian Churches** for they **were all wrong**, their creeds were an abomination in God's sight and their professors were all corrupt.[16]

After he received this vision, he said an angel named Moroni visited him and told him where to find some gold plates. These were the plates from which he was supposed to have translated the Book of Mormon.[17] He was also the one who was to perform the work of restoring the church to the earth.[18] So on April 6, 1830, Joseph Smith started his church known as The Church of Christ, later known as The Church of the Latter Day Saints, now known as The Church of Jesus Christ of Latter-day Saints.[19]

The early Mormon church leaders introduced several unique doctrines **never before found in Orthodox Christianity**. Their teachings included 1 - **polygamy** - the practice of having more than one wife at the same time, also stating that the God and Jesus Christ of Mormonism are polygamists,[7] 2 - **blood atonement** - the literal shedding of the blood of the sinner instead of relying on the shed Blood of the Saviour, Jesus Christ[20] and 3 - **their beliefs about God** - that there are millions of gods and that men may become gods.[2] One of my favorite statements was, "**As man is, God once was, as God is, man may become**."[21]

After the Nauvoo Expositor had exposed the teaching of the plurality of wives, Joseph Smith ordered the destruction of the printing press[22] and for this he was sentenced to the Carthage jail. While he was in jail a mob broke in and killed him. I was taught that he was a martyr, that he sealed his testimony with his blood, and that he said he was "led like a lamb to the slaughter."[23] As a Mormon, I compared his death to that of Jesus Christ's death on the cross. He was considered one of the saviors of mankind.[24]

History proved that Joseph Smith did not go like a lamb to the slaughter. He shot three men; killing two and injuring the third in a gun battle before he was shot.[25]

I IDOLIZED JOSEPH SMITH

I was never taught that he killed anyone. I was only taught the things that made him look wonderful. My teachers always seemed to leave out the facts, making him out to be more than just a mere human being. I placed him on a pedestal. He became the standard for what I wanted my husband to be, and his perfection was what I wished to achieve in my life. I idolized him as the man God had chosen to bring the gospel and the church back to the earth. Joseph Smith was more important to me than Jesus Christ. When I attended the LDS church, **our main focus was on Joseph Smith** and what he had done for us. I was taught that if it had not been for Joseph Smith, there would have been no salvation.[26] I was taught more about him and the Mormon "prophets" than any of the prophets in the Bible.

Even during our monthly fast and testimony meetings, almost everyone's testimony would speak of their belief that the LDS church was true and that Joseph Smith was a true prophet. **But seldom, if ever, were any praise or thanks given to the Lord for the sacrifice that Jesus Christ made on the cross for our sins**.

I was taught that the Bible was the Word of God as far as it was translated correctly.[27] I didn't want to read the Bible, because I did not know which part I could trust. The Book of Mormon, Doctrine and Covenants and Pearl of Great Price were the only books I needed, because Joseph Smith had written them, and I thought they were trustworthy.

CONVERTED TO MORMONISM ON MARCH 12, 1832

I was a sixth generation Mormon. My great, great, great grandfather, Milo Andrus, converted to Mormonism on March 12, 1832, just two years after the Mormon church began. He was acquainted with Joseph Smith and knew Brigham Young well. (Brigham Young later became the second "prophet" of the LDS church.) My grandpa Milo was present when the official announcement of the doctrine and practice of plural marriage was made. Although he did not want to live as a polygamist, Brigham Young told him it was required of him. He eventually took plural wives at the expense of his first wife and marriage, as his first wife would not live polygamy. He had a total of eleven wives and fifty-seven children.[28]

My family all belonged to this "only true church." My father and mother were very devout Mormons. My dad was a member of the High Council. He and my mother saw to it that

I attended church regularly, although I never had to be forced to go.

I Thought The World Of My Parents

Like most children, I thought the world of my parents. My dad was a truck driver, so I didn't get to see him very often. When he was home, he was either sleeping or reading. He had a set of the Journal of Discourses which contain the early Mormon teachings. This is what he read from most of the time. While reading these early LDS church writings, my dad's views started to change. He realized that **the Mormon church of today is not what it was like in the beginning**. Some of the doctrines had been changed and even their stand on who god is had changed.[29]

As a truck driver, my dad had several routes to southern Utah. This is where he met up with a group of Fundamentalist Mormons or Mormons who believe and practice the early teachings of Joseph Smith and Brigham Young and still live polygamy. He studied with them as often as he could. They expounded the early teachings and explained to him that they believed Wilford Woodruff the fourth "prophet" of the LDS church went astray by signing the Manifesto stopping polygamy.[30] They had broken away from the mainstream Mormon church and formed their own church with their own "prophet," yet they all still claim to be the "only true church."

"The New And Everlasting Covenant"

After spending time with this group, and after a lot of personal study, my dad thought it was only right that he become a polygamist. Brigham Young, the second "prophet" taught that only **those who become gods** are those who enter into polygamy.[31] Joseph Smith called polygamy the "New and **Everlasting** Covenant," and said that all those who are not living it would be dammed.[32]

One Day We Were a Happy Family...

While I was a child of eleven years of age, **my fifty-three year old father brought home a fifteen-year old girl** and told us that he must take her as his second wife in order to fulfill the law of eternal progression towards his own godhood. One day we were a happy family, and the next we were not; devastation struck our household. I thought she was my baby-sitter. Imagine my surprise when I learned she was going to be my "mother." I could not understand why my dad thought he needed another wife.

I had never heard my parents argue—until that night. My mother cried as my father tried to get her to accept this girl into our home. I laid in bed that night in horror, not knowing what the future would hold. I think my dad was surprised that my mother did not welcome this girl into our home with open arms. He had already settled it in his mind that he must live polygamy while it was a surprise to the rest of us. He had never told us of his secret meetings with this polygamous sect or of his findings as he studied the early Mormon doctrines.

Fear, hurt and anger hung over our house. My parents continued to fight, unable to settle their differences. And so, although I think my dad must have loved us, he left us, in order to follow the early LDS teachings.

After he moved out, he went to live in Colorado City, Arizona, which is a polygamist community. My dad "married" his second wife and a short time later "married" her sister, having a total of three wives.

My mother was left alone to raise her children. I was the youngest of her seven. I am now the seventh of sixteen children due to my dad's polygamous relationships. There were three of my mom's children still at home when he left.

My mother was very depressed after her husband left her. She had been hurt terribly. She had lived her life for her husband, who had **promised her everything — even eternity together**.*³³* She was so devastated over what had happened that it was hard for her to function. She stayed on the couch, unable to go on. I got myself to and from school with always the same result when I came home, she would be on the couch. My sisters and I had to take on several responsibilities that were sometimes hard to handle. But through this ordeal, it was my mom who was hurt the most. Although she did not agree with my dad taking plural wives, she did not divorce him.

She thought she still needed him, because Mormons are taught that it is the **men who call their wives out of the grave** and receives her into the celestial kingdom.*³⁴* (The highest level of the 3 degrees of the Mormon heavens.)

I was still very unsure as to why my dad thought he needed to "marry" other women. He said it was because he was being a true Mormon. I thought I was a true Mormon, but I had never been taught in my ward that I needed to live polygamy. (A ward is a name given to a local Mormon congregation.)

It was at this time that I knew I needed to find out for myself, what had actually been taught on this subject so that I could understand what had taken my dad away from me. I started to study on my own in the Book of Mormon. This was the book that Joseph Smith said was the "most correct book on the earth,"*³⁵* surely I would find my answers here. I continued to read until I found what I was looking for. The Book of Mormon states that polygamy was abominable (Mosiah 11:2 and Jacob

2:24) and that god commanded man to have only one wife and no concubines. (Jacob 2:27)

I was so excited! I had found something that would prove to my dad that what he was doing was wrong and he could come home. So, I wrote him a letter with the verses I had found that condemned polygamy, hoping that shortly I would see him come back home.

As time went by, and he had not responded, I became discouraged. Then one day, he wrote back. He thanked me for writing to him and showing him these passages, but he said that he must live the true gospel by living polygamy. He pointed out that in the Doctrine and Covenants - another book written by Joseph Smith - polygamy is called the "new and everlasting covenant"[32] and he said it must be fulfilled. He told me it did not matter what was written in the Book of Mormon, other revelation revealed that polygamy was now commanded and good in the sight of the god of Mormonism. He said I had better live it also or I would be damned.[32] I wondered, "Where would I be damned to?" I had never heard about hell and was never taught about a place of condemnation. It was taught that even the meanest sinner would find some place in the heavenly realm.[36] I knew then that I had lost my father to a set of man-made doctrines and ungodly practices that even contradicted his own scriptures.

A LIFE OF SECRECY

After my dad took plural wives, our lives took on a form of secrecy. I did not dare tell anyone where he had gone or what he had done. Polygamy was still illegal, although there are thousands living it daily. I was afraid he would get arrested and be sent to jail. I began to be very selective in the things I would say. **I became a very good liar**, deceiving all those who asked

9

me anything about him. Everything was a lie or a story. I never once felt any guilt for my actions, as I thought I was protecting him.

There were some people that knew what he had done and eventually most found out. We became outcasts. People, even some of our friends, became cold towards us. We were shunned by most of the members of the ward we belonged to. This was something I had a hard time understanding. After all, my dad was only following Mormon doctrine, yet most of our friends and family were embarrassed by it. Many Mormon people today are embarrassed by the doctrine of polygamy, many even deny it was taught. But the fact is, it was taught, believed and lived. Mormon doctrine states that polygamy will again be lived throughout eternity. For Mormon women who make it to the highest degree of heaven, they have only to look forward to sharing their husband with many other women for eternity.[37]

I NEVER ONCE QUESTIONED MY "CHURCH"

Even at the young age of eleven, I began to see the contradictions and problems with the Mormon accepted scriptures, but never once did I question the validity of the Mormon church. After all, from the time I could remember, I was told this was the only true church on the earth today, why would I question it?

Seeing how polygamy had destroyed my family, I didn't like that particular doctrine, yet I still loved the Mormon church. I believed the LDS church was true, but I knew it was time I got a "testimony" of its truthfulness for myself.

I was taught that I could know by a feeling that the Mormon church and the Book of Mormon was true and that Joseph Smith was a true prophet if I prayed about it. So, obeying the instructions I was given, that if I asked God with a sincere heart if this was true, then I would receive my answer from the Holy Spirit. I knelt down and prayed, being assured that if I asked in faith, I would receive my answer.[38] I then had the experience of having a "burning in my bosom." (Doctrine and Covenants 9:8) This is a supernatural manifestation that Mormons teach is the holy ghost testifying to the truthfulness of Mormonism. It is interesting to note that in the Bible, Jesus says that when the Holy Spirit is come, He will testify of Jesus Christ. (John 15:26) **NOT** a religious denomination.

My Zeal Continued to Grow

I now had a testimony of my own; my belief that this was the only true church was even stronger than before. As I got older, my zeal to serve in the Mormon church continued to grow. When I was a teenager, I was able to go to the Salt Lake Temple to be baptized for the dead. Mormonism teaches that in order to get into the celestial kingdom, you must first be baptized into the Mormon church. For those who have died without a Mormon baptism, someone has to stand in for them and be baptized by proxy.[39] This is the majority of the work performed in the LDS temples. I looked forward to this with great anticipation. Before I was allowed into the temple, I had to be interviewed by my bishop. He asked me several questions about my commitment to the LDS church, if I had been paying my tithes and if I had kept the word of wisdom, which is abstinence from coffee, tea, alcohol, tobacco, drugs and caffeine.[40] He also asked me several personal and embarrassing questions about my morality. Yet, I sat facing him, looking him in the eyes, knowing that I could truthfully answer these questions because I had kept myself morally clean.

What a sobering occasion for me as I walked through the temple doors knowing that I was one who was counted worthy to be doing work for the dead.[41] I was then baptized by immersion for about 20-30 dead people at a time.

MY SEMINARY TRAINING

When I was in the ninth grade, I was able to take my first year of LDS seminary. Almost every public junior high and high school in the state of Utah has an LDS seminary building adjacent to the school where the students are allowed time to go learn Mormon doctrine.

I enjoyed this very much. During my sophomore, junior, and senior years, I also took seminary where I was in the class presidencies. This was a great opportunity to get trained in the Mormon teachings.

One day during my seminary class, we had a guest speaker. He was dressed like a Catholic priest, but we were told he was a Baptist preacher. He told our class that we needed to be saved by grace and quoted Ephesians 2:8-9 from the Bible, *"For by grace are ye saved through faith; and that not of yourselves: it is the gift of God: Not of works, lest any man should boast."*

This was the first time I had heard these verses. I jumped up and quoted a passage out of the Book of Mormon, 2 Nephi 25:23, which states, "...it is by grace that we are saved, after all we can do." I told him that we have to do everything we can, and what we can't do, grace fills in. We had to work to get ourselves into heaven. The sacrifice that Jesus made on the cross was only for our physical resurrection.[42] If we wanted to get into the celestial kingdom we had to earn our own way.[33]

I LOVED MY RELIGION

My class and I debated with him on the Mormon teachings about salvation and exaltation into godhood. After our discussion, he said that he could see that what I was saying was the truth and that he must be converted to Mormonism. We were commended for my excellent proselytizing tactics and told I would make a good missionary. This boosted my confidence in my religion and myself.

It was only after class that I found out the man was really a returned Mormon missionary only playing the part to help train us. It didn't matter to me. I was happy knowing that I had succeeded in my first big lesson in converting someone to the LDS faith.

I loved my religion and was very self-righteous. I lived my religion to the fullest, loving the idea that my husband and I could someday be exalted to a god and goddess in heaven, thinking that I was well on my way to accomplish this. I was very proud to be a Mormon and I thought very highly of myself. There was no doubt in my mind that I would reach the celestial kingdom. I knew that I had been living up to the standards set forth by the LDS church. I attended church, paid my tithe, kept the word of wisdom, I was baptized for the dead and I dated only after the age of 16 and then it was only group dating. I was keeping myself morally clean so I could get married in the temple.

The goals I had set for myself were some that I knew I could achieve. The only man I wanted to marry would be a returned Mormon missionary and as righteous as I thought I was. We would go to the temple to be sealed together for eternity. Mormon doctrine claims that if a couple has a celestial or temple marriage, they will be married throughout eternity and continue to procreate and fill their own world. Civil or marriages performed outside the temples are until death or divorce only.[43]

It was my desire that my husband and I would continue to advance our positions of responsibility and prestige until eventually he would become the "prophet" and I would be the "prophet's" wife. This was a position I knew I could fill.

Throughout my life, I had been told I would be exalted, earning my own place in heaven, so I continued to work hard to insure my place in the highest level of heaven.

My Dreams Crashed

When I was a senior in high school, **I met my future husband**. He was not what I intended to marry. In fact, he was just the opposite. I met him one day when my Sunday school teacher (who was a returned Mormon missionary) was seen going into a house which was designated "off limits" to my girlfriends and I, because boys who drank and did drugs partied there. We knew we needed to rescue our teacher, so my friends and I went up to the house. There we saw our teacher smoking and drinking. I couldn't believe it.

We were met by four other boys who were also Mormon and three of them just happened to be in my ward. They were all smoking, drinking and doing drugs. I just assumed these guys needed someone to get them back into the LDS church and I thought I was just the one to do it.

This is how I met Richard. He was one of the boys who was drinking and doing drugs. I liked him instantly, but I knew if I were to date him, he would have to conform to the standards of the Mormon church. I then made it my duty to try to mold him into the perfect Mormon man I wanted him to be.

My girlfriends and I continued to spend time with them until we all became very good friends. At first it was easy for me to resist and refuse the alcohol and drugs. **But eventually my resistance wore down**.

Several of my ward members accused me of doing things with these guys and this made me mad. Up to this point I had never drank, taken drugs or even kissed Richard. But slowly, my high moral standards started to decline. Instead of molding Richard into what I wanted him to be, he began to reshape me. I started to drink. Not very much at first, then it got to where I couldn't wait for the weekends so we could get drunk.

I Graduated Into a Freefall of Sin

I finally graduated from high school and did not have to be under the watchful eye of my seminary teacher and classmates. **I was sliding downhill fast**. I didn't stop at alcohol; I also tried speed and cocaine. Richard and I went to the bars to dance and drink. I knew I was no longer the righteous girl I once thought I was. My dreams and goals were quickly slipping out of my reach.

I started attending cosmetology school during the day and working at night. All the while, I was falling deeper in love with Richard. Occasionally he would go to our ward with me, when his hangovers weren't too bad, which wasn't very often. I had stopped the drugs, but was still drinking. **I kept falling deeper into sin, although I never realized I was sinning against God**. I only thought I was being disobedient to the Mormon church.

As time went by, I eventually found out I was pregnant. My life became unbearable. Several people in my ward turned their back on me, others could only say, "I told you so." Some were nice, but not very many. Richard and I had been engaged for over a year and I thought our getting married would help bring back some of the respect I wished for. But we had been having some problems. I was stubborn and still wanted my temple marriage and **I blamed Richard for all of my failed dreams**. Richard despised me for feeling trapped into marriage and I resented him for everything that had happened to me. Because of this, we did not get married. Here I was, an unwed, pregnant Mormon girl. This was not how my life was supposed to turn out. How could this have happened to me?

I Cried Myself To Sleep

I finished cosmetology school and didn't want to do hair anymore, so I got a job in a day care. My heart broke as I took care of children who came from broken homes, for now, this was the same fate facing my own child.

Richard and I saw each other once in a while, but our families didn't make it any easier on us. Mine disliked him, his disliked me. **I cried myself to sleep night after night**; hating the circumstances which had brought me to this deep despair.

I only attended my ward once in a while now. I could not stand to see everyone's looks of pity and disappointment.

Finally after nine long months, I had my baby. How I wished that in the hospital before she was born, Richard and I would have been married, but it didn't happen. We had a beautiful little girl and I was now a single mother. Fear gripped my heart as I wondered how I could take care of my daughter.

My family was very good to me during this time. They helped me and gave me all the love and support I needed. But it wasn't enough. I wanted a husband and I wanted my daughter to know her father.

Richard was buying his own home so I moved in with him. He was a good father, but our living together did not solve any of our problems; it only made them worse. I had stopped drinking when I found out I was pregnant and was now trying to pull my life together.

Life was miserable for all of us. I had sunk so low into sin, that I could hardly stand myself. Gone were the days when I considered myself good enough to be a goddess over my own world.

Richard and I knew something needed to be done about our situation, so we got married. I wanted to have a big and beautiful wedding but we just appeared before a Justice of the Peace. Richard had gone to a party the night before we got married and got drunk, so drunk that he barely arrived at the courthouse that morning because he had a hangover.

Once again, this was nothing like I had envisioned for myself. **It was awful**. A few of our family members came but the day turned out to be a big disappointment for me. No beautiful dress, no bridesmaids, no walking down the aisle, no celebration, nothing fancy; just simply saying "I do" to a man who could barely stand up.

Life together was still terrible when I found out I was pregnant again. Richard and I still didn't like each other very much, but we were trying to make things work.

During this pregnancy, while I was about 5 months along, **Richard's life started to change**. He started to act differently. He stopped doing drugs and drinking. As soon as he came home from work he didn't run to the refrigerator for a beer. Instead he would say to me, "God loves you." This was not like him. My husband, who used to be more concerned with getting his next drink, was now telling me that God loved me.

Oh, Such Hurtful Words

I started to think that maybe he was finally willing to try to take me to the temple where our family could be sealed together forever. I thought it was all of my work in trying to get him to be a good Mormon that was now finally paying off. But then one day when Richard came home from work, he said something that altered the course of my life forever. He said, "Cindy, the Mormon church is not true, I cannot stay in it and I want you out of it, too."

Never had anyone spoken such hurtful words to me. The mere thought that my church might not be true outraged me. Who did he think he was to say this to me? How dare he even utter such words to me after he had crushed all of my dreams?

Life in our house became worse. Everyday when Richard would come home from work, he wanted to talk about the Mormon teachings. He would ask me questions about the early LDS doctrines. These were things I had never heard of such as: **the Jesus of Mormonism not being conceived by the Holy Ghost or born of a virgin, but conceived by a physical relationship between the god of Mormonism and his spiritual daughter Mary;**[44] **the fact that Joseph Smith had several "first" visions**[45] **and that his prophecies had failed.**[46] This was what Richard wanted to discuss with me. I was irrational, only responding with my testimony of the truthfulness of the LDS church. I did not have any answers as to why the doctrines had been changed or why the **Book of Mormon had almost 4000 changes made to it since it first came out in 1830**[47] or why the Book of Mormon which is supposed to be the "most correct" book on the earth, **does not contain the major doctrines of the Mormon church**. I could not answer why the **Mormon church does not use the Inspired Version**

of the Bible that Joseph Smith wrote. The only thing I could tell him was that he needed to talk to the Mormon missionaries, as I was not as smart as they were.

How could the LDS church not be true? After all, it contained the name of Jesus Christ right in the title of it. Everyday was the same thing. I couldn't wait for Richard to leave the house to go to work so I could be left alone. It would have been fine with me if he would have never come home. But each night he did and always to the same thing, more talk and more questions.

LIFE WITH RICHARD BECAME UNBEARABLE

Everyday Richard would bring me home literature about the problems with the Mormon teachings. I was so angry; telling him it was all Anti-Mormon literature, never taking the time to read that it was all **material taken out of LDS sources**. Biblical Gospel tracts were dispersed throughout our house so I would find them. He brought movies home for me to watch and tapes for me to listen to. I was going crazy; I could not stand it anymore. I was mad at Richard all the time. I did not want to live like this any longer.

But the most remarkable thing that occurred during this time was the change in Richard. Even though I hated him and was so angry at him, I could see how he was changing. He no longer listened to rock music, he stopped cursing, his want for alcohol ceased and he had a genuine love for our family. He was no longer angry all the time. He was a different person.

Richard had been working with a man who was a Christian and he had been showing Richard the changes in the LDS teachings and talking to him about the Bible and the Jesus Christ of the Bible. **Richard** had realized his need for the Saviour. He had stopped trusting in himself and his religion and **had received the Lord Jesus Christ** into his heart and life as his personal Lord and Saviour and was born-again becoming a Christian.

Even still, I hated my husband. Life with him was terrible. I had just had our second child, another beautiful little girl, when I decided I couldn't live like this any more. I was so angry with Richard for telling me that the Mormon church was not true, after all, he had been raised Mormon all of his life, too. Some of the leaders of our ward came to our house and counseled me to leave him and to find someone who was a faithful Mormon who would be willing to take me to the temple. I decided this would be the best thing for everyone involved. I found a name, number and address of a divorce lawyer and was going to end this marriage.

I WILL PROVE RICHARD WRONG

The only vehicle we had was a truck with a stick-shift which I had a hard time driving. I sat in the truck with the lawyer's address in my hand, ready to go, but I couldn't put the truck in reverse to get out of the driveway. I was furious! I was so angry by this time, that the only thought that came to mind was that I could not leave with Richard thinking he was right. I had to prove to him that the Mormon church was true. Then he would have to apologize to me for all these months of misery. A new plan started to form in my mind. I would find the answers to all of the questions he had asked and **show him that I was right and he was wrong**.

I went to the library and checked out every book I could find on the early LDS church history and doctrines. I studied during all of my spare time trying to find something that would support my claims. The more I studied, the more I realized how little I really knew about my religion. **Instead of finding**

the answers I was looking for, **I found more questions and problems**.

I saw how some of the major doctrines had been changed. When polygamy was given it was essential to salvation,[48] and now it was no longer required.[30] Adam was the god of Mormonism at one time and it was called scripture by Brigham Young[49] and now it is called false doctrine by the twelfth "prophet" of the LDS church, Spencer W. Kimball.[50] The black people at one time were called an inferior race[51] and told they were unworthy and unable to hold the Mormon priesthood.[52] Yet, on June 9, 1978, in the <u>Deseret News</u>, Spencer W. Kimball, announced that by "revelation" the black people could now hold the Mormon priesthood. (Also found in the <u>Official Declaration–2</u>) Although my dad, after studying the early church doctrines became a polygamist, I did not know what I should do. **Which "prophet" should I follow?**

I read many prophecies that Joseph Smith gave that did not come to pass. What really scared me was, after **Joseph Smith gave a particular revelation** that the copyright of the Book of Mormon would be sold in Canada, **his prophecy failed completely**. His explanation was, **"Some revelations are of God: some revelations are of man: and some revelations are of the devil."** (<u>An Address To All Believers In Christ</u> by David Whitmer, pp. 30-31) And here I was trusting my eternal existence on someone who did not even know who his revelations were coming from!

I read how the blood atonement doctrine was put into actual practice, and how people lost their lives by having their throat slit from ear to ear to allow their blood to be spilt to atone for their sins.[53] And in the temple ceremony, all those who participate, make oaths to remind themselves of what will happen to them if they reveal the secrets that are performed in there. During one part of the temple ceremony, the participants are instructed to place their green, fig leaf apron around their waist which a man portraying **Lucifer just revealed was an "emblem of <u>his</u> power and priesthoods."**[54]

I read about **Joseph Smith's** history, of his claim of "knowing more than all the world put together,"[55] and his **boasting of doing greater things than Jesus.**[56] I learned how he was involved in the occult by using divining rods and claiming to use a seer stone in translating the Book of Mormon.[57]

However, the thing that scared me the most, after I really started to read the Christian Gospel tracts and my Bible, was that I realized the **Mormon church's teachings and the Bible do not go hand in hand** like I had been taught. Mormonism was in direct opposition to what the God of the Bible has spoken. I did not dare tell Richard of my discoveries just yet. I was scared. What was I trusting in for my eternal life? I did not know what to believe.

One day while Richard was at work; I got out one of the papers he had brought home for me to read. It had a picture of a Christian missionary family who had given their lives (not just two years) to serve God. They gave their testimony about their love and gratitude for Jesus, thanking Him for saving their souls. Their love for the Saviour was so real and genuine. **My heart longed to know this Jesus** whom they were speaking about. I did not know Him as I only knew of a Jesus who was my brother and example, and I could be just as good as him if I tried. As a Mormon, I never gave my worship and adoration to the Lord. All of my love and devotion went to Joseph Smith and the Mormon church. But now, **I wanted to know this Jesus who could save my soul**.

During this time of my research, Richard's and my life was still horrible. Richard was changing, getting kinder and happier all the time. I was getting angrier, still trying to hold on to the belief that the Mormon church was true. I thought that maybe the problems were with the people and not the LDS church itself. But the more I studied, the more I realized there were **too many contradictions and changes for it to be true**.

RICHARD TOLD ME OF THE RAPTURE - IT SCARED ME TO DEATH

Richard had been speaking to his co-worker about a subject that I had never heard of before; it was called the **"Rapture."** The Rapture is described in 1 Thessalonians 4:16-17,

> *"For the Lord himself shall descend from heaven with a shout, with the voice of the archangel, and with the trump of God: and the dead in Christ shall rise first: Then we which are alive and remain shall be caught up together with them in the clouds, to meet the Lord in the air: and so shall we ever be with the Lord."*

One day when Richard came home from work, he told me something that really scared me. He said, "When the Rapture occurs, me and our two girls will be gone, but you will be left behind." Not only did this scare me, but it confused me. I had never heard about the Rapture. And who was Richard to say I could not go? I had always lived a better life than he had, surely I could go. I was still so angry at Richard that it would not have mattered to me where he went, but I did not want my daughters going anywhere without me. Even though I did not believe what Richard had said, I was scared, **I did not want to be left behind**.

All through my childhood, I had been taught that the Mormon church was the only true church. But I knew I needed to seriously reconsider what I was basing my eternal life on. I wanted what that Christian missionary family and Richard had. Richard's life had been completely changed and I knew it was

not a religion that had made the difference, he was not even attending church at the time. **It was a personal relationship with the Jesus Christ of the Bible.**

A Beautiful Cover

While I was searching for the answers I so desperately wanted, I picked up a book from off of our bookshelf titled, **"God's Word, Final, Infallible and Forever."** This book had been left on our doorstep about one year prior to this and the only reason Richard kept it was it had a nice landscape cover. Our Christian neighbor up the street had left this book at our house during an outreach in our area. This book was written to show the validity of the Bible as the Word of God and some of the problems with the Mormon teachings.

The first section of this book told about the Bible being the only Word of God and explained how the God of the Bible is All Powerful and is able to keep His Word pure for us today. I learned how there are **no errors in the Bible** and that **it is trustworthy.** This was something I had never heard before as I had always been taught that the Bible had been mistranslated[27] and that there were many plain and precious parts taken out.[58] Yet, this information was very exciting to me as I thought about there being a **God who is powerful enough to preserve His Word for me today in the King James Version.** (Matthew 24:35; Psalm 12:6-7; 2 Timothy 3:16; 1 Peter 1:23-25)

The next section told of some of the problems in the Mormon teachings. These were some of the things I had already been studying and this reinforced the doubts I had. There was also a biblical plan of salvation. It was so wonderful and simple that I thought it was too easy. How could I just **believe on and receive Jesus Christ for my salvation?**

I remembered the verses quoted to me from the man who pretended to be a Baptist preacher from my seminary class. (Ephesians 2:8-9) I knew if I would be able to get to heaven on my own, then I would boast for all eternity about all the good works I had done to get myself there and that would be unacceptable to God. I didn't want to trust my way anymore; I wanted God's way.

I Knew I Was a Sinner

First, I had to realize I was a sinner. The Bible says, *"As it is written, There is none righteous, no, not one:"* (Romans 3:10) *"For all have sinned, and come short of the glory of God;"* (Romans 3:23) Before I had met Richard, I never thought I had sinned. I was the epitome of perfection in my own mind. But after I met Richard, I did drugs, I drank, I ended up an unwed mother and I was angry all the time. Yes, I now knew I was a sinner. I had been brought down to the lowest point in my life. I had sinned against a Holy and Righteous God.

A Lake of Fire Forever!

Next the Bible said there was a penalty for my sin and that penalty was a burning lake of fire forever. *"For the wages of sin is death;..."* (Romans 6:23a) *"And death and hell were cast into the lake of fire. This is the second death."* (Revelation 20:14)

"But the fearful, and unbelieving, and the abominable, and murderers, and whoremongers, and sorcerers, and idolaters, and all liars, shall have their part in the lake which burneth with fire and brimstone: which is the second death." (Revelation 21:8)

25

Well, I had never heard that. But I knew I deserved this, I had sinned. The Bible said that Jesus had died to pay for my sin. When He died on that old, cruel cross almost two thousand years ago, my sins were placed on Him. **Jesus died so I might live**. *"But God commendeth his love toward us, in that, while we yet sinners, Christ died for us."* (Romans 5:8)

I had always heard that Jesus died for me, but I was told it was only for my physical resurrection, I had to work to get myself into heaven. Then I started to wonder, **"How much work would it take?"** Even if I repented and went back to the LDS church faithfully, went through the temple, paid my tithe and did my work for the dead, would it be enough? How would I know when I had done all I needed to do? I wondered if when I died and stood before God, He would say I was $1.00 short on my tithe or I missed one week too many of church. Then I could not get into the degree of heaven I desired to attain. How would I know?

The Jesus of the Bible died not only for my physical resurrection, but also for the salvation of my spirit and soul. He is able to forgive **all** of my sins and save me. *"Wherefore he is able also to save them to the uttermost that come unto God by him,..."* (Hebrews 7:25)

As a Mormon, I was taught that it was baptism that washed away my sins and I had been baptized at the age of eight. Can you imagine all of the sins I had accumulated since then? Mormon doctrine also states that once I repented, **if I sinned again, every previous sin would come back**.[59] This was terrible. If God would not allow sin into His Heaven, then I would not be allowed in.

I never knew that I was a sinner in need of a Saviour, because I thought I could get into heaven on my own merit. But Jesus said, *"...I am the way, the truth, and the life: no man cometh unto the Father, but by me."* (John 14:6) I finally started to understand that it was only Jesus who could get me into heaven, not my church, my water baptism, or all of the wonderful good works I could perform could get me into God's Heaven. The Bible says "*...all our righteousnesses are as filthy rags;...*" (Isaiah 64:6) The Bible also says, "*Not by works of righteousness which we have done, but according to his mercy he saved us,...*" (Titus 3:5) **It is only by the Blood of Jesus Christ that we can have forgiveness of sin**. "*...and the blood of Jesus Christ his Son cleanseth us from all sin.*" (1 John 1:7) "*...Unto him that loved us, and **washed us from our sins in his own blood**,*" (Revelation 1:5) "*In whom we have **redemption through his blood**, even the forgiveness of sins:*" (Colossians 1:14)

A FREE GIFT FROM GOD

The Bible says that salvation is a gift from God. "*...but the gift of God is eternal life through Jesus Christ our Lord.*" (Romans 6:23b) A gift is something that I did not have to work for, only acknowledge it was being offered and receive it. I finally realized I was a sinner, recognizing the penalty for my sin and understood that I could not get myself into heaven. **By faith I needed to trust Jesus Christ alone, plus and minus nothing,** and ask Him to forgive me and save me.

> "*That if thou shalt confess with thy mouth the Lord Jesus, and shalt believe in thine heart that God hath raised him from the dead, thou shalt be saved. For with the heart man believeth unto righteousness; and with the mouth confession is made unto salvation....For whosoever shall call upon the name of the Lord shall be saved.*" (Romans 10:9-10, 13)

MY MANY STRUGGLES ENDED IN PEACE

I now knew my religion could never get me into heaven. In the book I was reading, after the biblical plan of Salvation, was a sinner's prayer. I went into my bedroom and knelt down by my bed and simply read the prayer as it was written in the book. As soon as I had prayed and asked the God of the Bible to forgive me and asked Jesus Christ to come into my heart and life and save me, **my life was changed forever**. I then realized I had been wandering around in spiritual darkness all of my life. But when I trusted Jesus Christ alone as my Saviour, my eyes were opened and I could see. I came out of the darkness and into His marvelous light. (1 Peter 2:9) I knew at that moment that everything I had been raised with and had been trusting in for my eternal life was wrong. I knew then that it was **not a religion that would get me into heaven but only a relationship with Jesus Christ**. This was the prayer I prayed:

> **"Lord Jesus Christ, come into my heart and life. Cleanse me from all my sin by your shed blood. Make me a child of God. Give me your free gift of everlasting life, and let me know I am saved, now and forever. I now receive you as my very own personal Lord and Saviour, in Jesus' name, Amen."**

My life had been changed in a moment. I now had a personal relationship with the Living Lord, Jesus Christ. I had been forgiven, saved and born again into God's family, becoming His child. (John 1:12; Ephesians 1:5) I knew **salvation was instantaneous and not a process of works**. (Romans 6:23; 10:9-10, 13; Ephesians 2:8-9)

I had to tell someone, so I told Richard. I had to admit that I had been wrong. But that didn't matter. I now had peace and I knew for certain where I would go if the Rapture occurred or when I died. I would be in heaven with Jesus, not because of anything that I have done, but because of everything that Jesus has done.

WE STARTED TO REBUILD OUR MARRIAGE

By the Grace of God, Richard and I started to rebuild our life together. It was only by that grace that we are still married because of the bitterness and resentment we had for each other. It has taken time, but God has restored our love for each other and has even given me a greater love and deeper respect for my husband.

We knew it was time that we told our families that we were no longer attending the LDS church. We had hoped that they would be happy that someone was finally sharing the truth with them from the Bible. Were we ever wrong! They had the same reaction with us that I had with Richard — anger, resentment and unbelief. Our families couldn't understand how we could do this to them.

Our hearts break for our friends and family as we know the bondage they are under trying to live up to the expectations of thinking they can become a god. It cannot be done, **there is only one God and no one will ever become one**. (Deut. 4:35, 39, 6:4; Isaiah 43:10-11, 44:6, 8, 45:5-6, 18, 21-22, 46:9; Psalm 86:10; Mark 12:29, 32; 1 Timothy 2:5; 1 John 5:7)

In the Bible, Genesis chapter 3, it was **Satan who first introduced the doctrine that man could become as god**.

"And the serpent said unto the woman, Ye shall not surely die: For God doth know that in the day ye eat

*thereof, then your eyes shall be opened, **and ye shall be as gods,...**"*

This is Satan's number one doctrine. It was because of this belief that Satan was cast out of heaven. (Isaiah 14:12-15) All creation was cursed because of the fall of man. It was not a fall upward as Mormonism teaches.[60]

WE ARE NOT ATTACKING - WE ARE DEFENDING

Please understand that we are not attacking anyone. In Jude 3 it tells us to, "...*earnestly contend for the faith which was **once** delivered unto the saints*." We are defending the Lord Jesus Christ and His Promise not only that He established His Church, but also His Promise to keep and preserve His Church. "*And I say also unto thee, That thou art Peter, and upon this rock **I will build my church; and the gates of hell shall not prevail against it**.*" Matthew 16:18 (1 Corinthians 3:11; Ephesians 2:20; Acts 2:47; Jude 3; 1 Peter 1:25)

The LDS church was started because Joseph Smith claimed that all Christian Churches were wrong, their creeds were an abomination in god's sight and their professors were all corrupt.[61] It was also stated that the Church that Jesus Christ started and promised to preserve had gone into apostasy and that Joseph Smith was called to restore it.[62]

Joseph Smith said the church fell away and needed to be restored. The Lord Jesus Christ said not even the gates of hell would prevail against His Church.

WHICH ONE WILL YOU BELIEVE – JOSEPH SMITH OR JESUS CHRIST?

"Unto him be glory in the church by Christ Jesus throughout all ages, world without end. Amen." (Ephesians 3:21)

It is our utmost desire that all who read this book will understand that we are all sinners deserving God's judgment of death and hell, yet recognize the payment for our sin debt has been paid in full by Jesus Christ and His sacrifice on the cross. The Lord offers this to all who will repent of their sins, asking the Lord to forgive them and trust in Jesus Christ's death, burial and resurrection for salvation of their soul.

"For God so loved the world that he gave his only begotten Son, that whosoever believeth in him, should not perish, but have everlasting life." (John 3:16)

"For whosoever shall call upon the name of the lord, shall be saved." (Romans 10:13)

TERMINOLOGY DIFFERENCE

Be aware: biblical terms may be used, but having a different meaning. You may want to ask, "What do you mean by being 'Born-Again?'" etc.

PRE-EXISTENCE:

LDS - Believes that everyone existed as spirit children in heaven with god the Father and have always existed.

BIBLE - Only God has always existed. (Gen. 1:1; Ps. 90:2)

SONS OF GOD:

LDS - We are all literal spiritual children of God. Jesus and Lucifer are spirit brothers.

BIBLE - We become a child of God when we are born again. (John 1:12)

BORN-AGAIN:

LDS - Water Baptism into the LDS Church

BIBLE - We are spiritually dead until our spiritual birth by faith in Jesus Christ as our personal Lord and Saviour. (Eph. 2:1, 8-9; John 3:8; 1 Peter 1:23)

GOSPEL:

LDS - The Mormon Church system and doctrines

BIBLE - Jesus Christ died for our sins, was buried and rose again the third day according to the Scriptures as payment for all mans sin. Which payment is applied to all that personally accepts Him as their Saviour. (1 Corinthians 15:1-4; 1 Corinthians 1:17-18; Romans 5:6, 8)

AUTHORITY-PRIESTHOOD:

LDS - Believe that only LDS have authority to baptize, ordain, etc. Having a two part system of priesthood – Melchizedek and Aaronic.

BIBLE - Christ brought an end to the Levital (Aaronic) Priesthood, and is the ONLY High Priest after the order of Melchisedec. (Hebrews 6:8)

Each believer is considered part of the royal priesthood. (1 Peter 3:9)

SCRIPTURE:

LDS - Their standard works accepted as scripture: The King James Bible as far as it is translated correctly (trusted only when it agrees with Mormonism). The Book of Mormon, The Doctrine and Covenants and the Pearl of Great Price. Living LDS prophet held superior to everything else.

BIBLE - The Holy Bible is God's perfectly preserved Word. The only Holy Spirit inspired book from which God has given us to know Him, His will and His way of Salvation. Preserved for the English speaking people in the King James Version. (2 Timothy 3:16; 2 Peter 1:20-21; Isaiah 40:8; Matthew 24:35)

GODHEAD:

LDS - Three totally separate gods. Jesus and god the Father have physical bodies, the holy ghost a spirit body; holy spirit is an influence.

BIBLE - Only one God (Isaiah 44:8, 45:5-6, 18, 21-22; 1 John 5:7) He is a Spirit (John 4:24) And NOT an exalted man (Numbers 23:19)

HEAVEN:

LDS - Divided into three kingdoms, Celestial, Terrestrial, and Telestial. (See graphic on following page.)

BIBLE - For all born again children of God. A literal place where God dwells. (John 14:1-6; Rev. 21:9-27) Only mentions two conditions: Everlasting punishment (2nd death) or Eternal life (Matthew 25:31-46)

The Mormon Idea of Heaven

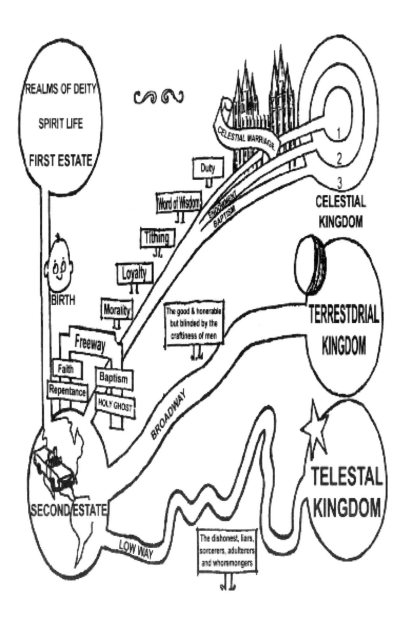

The Way of the Cross

"For the preaching of the cross is to them that perish foolishness: but unto us which are saved it is the power of God." (1 Corinthians 1:18)

COMPARISONS

**"TAKE UP THE BIBLE,
COMPARE THE RELIGION OF THE
LATTER-DAY SAINTS
WITH IT, AND SEE IF IT WILL STAND THE TEST."**
Brigham Young, Journal of Discourses, Vol. 16, p. 46

The Following Pages List Some
Comparisons Between
The Bible and LDS Teachings

Mormonism Says

Mormonism Encourages You To...

"...**learn to do as you are told**...if you are told by your leader
to do a thing, do it.
None of your business whether it is right or wrong."
Journal of Discourses, Vol. 6, p. 32

"...Lucifer...wins a great victory when he can get the
members of the Church to speak against their
leaders and do their own thinking..."
Improvement ERA, 1924

Many, even Millions of gods

"...you have got to learn how to be Gods yourselves,...
the same as all Gods have done before you,..."
Teachings of the Prophet Joseph Smith
by Joseph Fielding Smith, p. 346

"Brethren, 225,000 of you are here tonight.
I suppose 225,000 of you may become gods..."
Spencer W. Kimball, Ensign, Nov. 1975, p. 80

"If we should take a million of worlds like this and
number their particles, we should find that there
are more Gods than there are particles
of matter in those worlds."
Orson Pratt, Journal of Discourses, Vol. 2, p. 345

The Bible Says

The God of the Bible Encourages You To...

*"**Prove all things**; hold fast that which is good."*
(1 Thessalonians 5:21)

*"**Study** to shew thyself approved unto God,..."*
(2 Timothy 2:15)

*"...**Ye do err, not knowing the scriptures**,
nor the power of God."* (Matthew 22:29)

The Bible warns about how to **test false prophets**.
1st - If their **prophecies fail**. **2nd** - If they **lead you to
worship other gods**. You are not to fear or follow them.
(Deuteronomy 13:1-11, 18:20-22 and Exodus 20:3)
**Is the God of the Bible the same
as the God of Mormonism?**

Only One God

*"...I am he: **before me there was no God formed, neither
shall there be after me**. I, even I, am the LORD;..."*
(Isaiah 43:10-11)

"...I am the first, and I am the last;..." (Isaiah 44:6)

*"Look unto me, and be ye saved, all the ends of the earth: for
I am God, and there is none else."* (Isaiah 45:22)

Mormonism Says

Men Can and Have Become Gods

"As man is, God once was, as God is, man may become."
Lorenzo Snow, <u>Millennial Star</u>, Vol. 54, p. 404

"...man is the offspring of God;...having within
him the seeds of godhood and thus being
a god in embryo,..."
<u>Miracle of Forgiveness</u> by Spencer W. Kimball, p. 3

"...**We are created,...to become Gods**..."
Brigham Young, <u>Journal of Discourses</u>, Vol. 3, p. 93

God is an Exalted Man

"God himself is an exalted man, perfected,
enthroned and supreme."
Joseph Fielding Smith, <u>Improvement ERA</u>,
Vol. 13, p. 81

"The Father has a body of flesh and bones as
tangible as man's;..."
<u>Doctrines and Covenants 130:22</u>

"God himself, the Father of us all, is a glorified,
exalted, immortal, resurrected Man!"
<u>Mormon Doctrine</u> by Bruce R. McConkie, p. 643

The Bible Says

Man is not, nor ever will be a god

"God is not a man, that he should lie;
neither the son of man, that he should repent:..."
(Numbers 23:19)

"...for I am God, and not man;..." (Hosea 11:9)

"...for I am God, and there is none else; I am God, and there
is none like me," (Isaiah 46:9)

It is important to note that is was Satan who first
introduced this lie through the serpent to mankind
that man could become as god. (Gen. 3) It was this
same sin that got him, (Lucifer) cast out of heaven,
whose destiny is the lake of fire. (Isaiah 14 and Rev. 20)

God is a Spirit

"God is a Spirit: and they that worship him must worship him
in spirit and in truth." (John 4:24)

"...a spirit hath not flesh and bones, as ye see me have."
(Luke 24:39)

"Professing themselves to be wise, they became fools, And
changed the glory of the uncorruptible God into an image
made like to corruptible man,..." (Romans 1:22-23)

Mormonism Says

The Jesus of Mormonism

Not conceived of the Holy Ghost, but by a physical relationship of the Mormon god, who is an exalted man.
"Now, remember from this time forth, and for ever that, **Jesus Christ was not begotten by the Holy Ghost.**"
Brigham Young, <u>Journal of Discourses</u>, Vol. 1, p. 51

"Christ was begotten of God. He was not born without the aid of Man, and that Man was God!"
<u>Doctrines of Salvation</u> by Joseph Fielding Smith, Vol. 1, p. 18

Jesus and God the Father are Polygamists
"We have now clearly shown that God the Father had a plurality of wives, one or more being in eternity,...
We have also proved that both God the Father and our Lord Jesus Christ inherit their wives in eternity..."
<u>The Seer</u> by Orson Pratt, Nov. 1883, p. 172

"The only men who become Gods, even the Sons of God, are those who enter into polygamy."
Brigham Young, <u>Journal of Discourses</u>, Vol. 11, p. 269
(Brigham Young stated that **every sermon he preached was to be accepted as scripture**. <u>Journal of Discourses</u>, Vol. 13, p. 95)

Mormonism Worships a Different Christ
"...the Christ followed by the Mormons **is not** the Christ followed by traditional Christianity."
Elder Benard P. Brockbank, <u>The Ensign</u>, May 1977, p. 26

"In bearing testimony of Jesus Christ, President Hinckley spoke of those outside the Church who say Latter-day Saints 'do not believe in the traditional Christ.'
'No, I don't. The traditional Christ of whom they speak is not the Christ of whom I speak.'"
Gordon B. Hinckley, <u>LDS Church News</u>, week ending June 20, 1998, p. 7

THE BIBLE SAYS

THE LORD JESUS HIMSELF WARNED;

"...Take heed that no man deceive you. For many shall come in my name,...and shall deceive many." (Matthew 24:4-5)

Is the Jesus of the Bible the same as the Jesus of Mormonism?

THE JESUS OF THE BIBLE

Born of a Virgin and Conceived by the Holy Ghost
"Now the birth of Jesus Christ was on this wise: When as his mother Mary was espoused to Joseph, before they came together, she was found with child of the Holy Ghost." (Matthew 1:18)
(See also Isaiah 7:14 and Luke 1:26-35)

Not Married
Jesus attended a marriage at Cana,
but only as a guest. (John 2:1-11).

There are no references in the Bible that
God The Father or Jesus were ever married.

If marriage and/or polygamy were such an important issue,
then God would have given many indications that He was
married, to one and/or multiple wives.

Jesus warns, *"For there shall arise false Christs, And false prophets, and shall shew great signs and wonders;... Behold, I have told you before."* (Matthew 24:24-25)

43

MORMONISM SAYS

THE MORMON JESUS IS UNABLE TO SAVE

"The world should know that since the
Lord himself cannot save men in their sins,..."
Miracle of Forgiveness by Spencer W. Kimball, p. 167

"...we are the only people that know how to save our
progenitors, how to save ourselves, and how to save our
posterity...we in fact are the saviours of the world,..."
John Taylor, Journal of Discourses, Vol. 6, p. 163

"If it had not been for Joseph Smith and the restoration, there
would be no salvation. There is no salvation outside The
Church of Jesus Christ of Latter-day Saints."
Mormon Doctrine by Bruce R. McConkie, p. 670

THE MORMON GOSPEL

"We believe that the first principles and ordinances of the
Gospel are: first, Faith in the Lord Jesus Christ;
second, Repentance; third, Baptism by immersion
for the remissions of sins;..."
4th Article of Faith of the LDS Church

"...a code of laws and commandments whereby we might
attain perfection and, eventually, godhood. This set of laws
and ordinances is known as the gospel of Jesus Christ, and it
is the only plan which will exalt mankind. The Church of
Jesus Christ of Latter-day Saints is the sole repository
of this priceless program..."
Miracle of Forgiveness by Spencer W. Kimball, p. 6

The Bible Says

The Jesus of the Bible is the One and Only Saviour of Mankind

"For unto you is born this day in the city of David a Saviour, which is Christ the Lord." (Luke 2:11)

"Jesus saith unto him, I am the way, the truth, and the life: no man cometh unto the Father, but by me." (John 14:6)

"Neither is there salvation in any other: for there is none other name under heaven given among men, whereby we must be saved." (Acts 4:12)

"...Christ Jesus came into the world to save sinners;..." (1 Timothy 1:15)

The Gospel

We have **another Biblical warning** here about those who would preach **another gospel**. *"...but there be some that trouble you, and would pervert the gospel of Christ. But though we, **or an angel** from heaven, preach any other gospel unto you than that which we have preached unto you, **let him be accursed**."* (Galatians 1:7-9)

*"...I declare unto you the **gospel** which I preached...**By which also ye are saved**,...how that Christ died for our sins according to the scriptures; And that he was buried, and that he rose again the third day according to the scriptures."* (1 Corinthians 15:1-4)

*"For Christ sent me **not to baptize**, but to preach the gospel:..."* (1 Corinthians 1:17)

45

MORMONISM SAYS

SALVATION BY WORKS, FAITH AND GRACE

"One of the most fallacious doctrines originated by
Satan and propounded by man is that man is saved
alone by the grace of God;..."
Miracle of Forgiveness by Spencer W. Kimball, p. 206

"...for we know that it is by grace that we are saved,
after all we can do." Book of Mormon, 2 Nephi 25:23

"That by keeping the commandments they might be washed
and cleansed from all their sins,..."
Doctrine of Covenants 76:52

TWO TYPES OF SALVATION IN MORMONISM
General
"...general salvation,...consists in the mere
fact of being resurrected."
"Immortality is a free gift and comes without works or
righteousness of any sort; all men will come forth in the
resurrection because of the atoning sacrifice of
Christ...Immortality comes by grace alone, but those who
gain it may find themselves damned in eternity."
Mormon Doctrine by Bruce R. McConkie, p. 669 and 671

Individual
"...that which comes by grace coupled with gospel
obedience,...This kind of salvation follows faith, repentance,
baptism, receipt of the Holy Ghost, and continued
righteousness to the end of one's mortal probation."
Mormon Doctrine by Bruce R. McConkie, p. 669-670

THE BIBLE SAYS

SALVATION BY GRACE THROUGH FAITH

"For by grace are ye saved through faith; and that not of yourselves: it is the gift of God: Not of works, lest any man should boast." (Ephesians 2:8-9)

"Knowing that a man is not justified by the works of the law, but by the faith of Jesus Christ,...for if righteousness come by the law, then Christ is dead in vain." (Galatians 2:16, 21)

The Lord Jesus shared many good examples of God's grace to sinful man...

In Luke 18:9-14 Jesus spoke of two men that went to the temple to pray. A Pharisee and a publican. The Pharisee was a very religious man who had a **special priesthood, special garments, a temple** and did many religious works. The publican was a tax collector, many times extorting money from those he collected taxes from. The Pharisee gloried in his religious works. The publican, humbly asked, **"God be merciful to me a sinner."** And Jesus said that it was the publican that went home justified or forgiven that day, not the religious Pharisee. (Also see Luke 23:32-43)

"Being justified freely by his grace through the redemption that is in Christ Jesus:" (Romans 3:24)

Mormonism Says

The Blood of Jesus Christ is Not Sufficient to Cleanse Us From Sin

"Joseph Smith taught that there were **certain sins** so grievous that man may commit, that they will place the transgressors **beyond the power of the atoning blood of Christ**. If these offenses are committed, then the blood of Christ will not cleanse them from their sins even though they repent. Therefore **their only hope is to have their own blood shed to atone**, as far a possible, in their behalf."
Doctrines of Salvation by Joseph Fielding Smith, Vol. 1, p. 135

Sin Is Washed Away By Water Baptism

"Baptism...It is for the remission of sins."
Mormon Doctrine by Bruce R. McConkie, p. 70

"...Baptism by immersion for the remission of sins;..."
LDS 4th Article of Faith

"There is no salvation outside the Church of Jesus Christ of Latter-day Saints."
Mormon Doctrine, p. 670

THE BIBLE SAYS

IT IS THE BLOOD OF JESUS CHRIST THAT CLEANSES US FROM ALL SIN

*"...**it is the blood** that maketh an atonement for the soul."*
(Leviticus 17:11)

*"...**without shedding of blood is no remission**."*
(Hebrews 9:22)

*"In whom we have **redemption through his blood**,
the forgiveness of sins,..."* (Ephesians 1:7)

*"In whom we have **redemption through his blood**,
even the forgiveness of sins:"* (Colossians 1:14)

*"...and the **blood of Jesus Christ his Son
cleanseth us from all sin**."* (1 John 1:7)

*"...Unto him that loved us, and **washed us
from our sins in his own blood**,"* (Revelation 1:5)

*"Forasmuch as ye know that ye were **not redeemed** with
corruptible things,...received **by tradition from your fathers;
But with the precious blood of Christ**,..."* (1 Peter 1:18-19)

Mormonism Says

Joseph Smith Stated He Did Greater Works Than Jesus

"...I have more to boast of than ever any man had. I am the only man that has ever been able to keep a whole church together...Neither Paul, John, Peter, nor Jesus ever did it. **I boast that no man ever did such a work as I**."
History of the Church, Vol. 6, p. 408-409

"...I am learned, and know more than all the world put together."
Journal of Discourses, Vol. 6, p. 5

Concerning the Blacks

"...the Lord God did cause a skin of blackness to come upon them. And thus saith the Lord God: I will cause that they shall be loathsome..."
Book of Mormon, 2 Nephi 5:21-22

"And the **skins** of the Lamenites **were dark**, according to the mark which was set upon their fathers, **which was a curse upon them because of their transgressions**..."
Book of Mormon, Alma 3:6

Concerning His Failed Prophecies

When one of Joseph Smiths prophecies failed, he stated about his own prophecies, "**Some revelations are of God**: some revelations are of man: **and some revelations are of the devil**."
An Address To All Believers In Christ
by David Whitmer, pp. 30-31

Why would any one trust their eternal destiny on a man who claimed to be a prophet of God, **yet did not know** when his prophecies were from God, man or the devil?

THE BIBLE SAYS

JESUS SAID...

*"Take my yoke upon you, and learn of me; **for I am meek and lowly in heart**: and ye shall find rest unto your souls."*
(Matthew 11:29)

*"For whosoever **exalteth** himself shall be abased;"*
(Luke 14:11)

CONCERNING HOW GOD LOOKS AT MAN

*"...for the LORD seeth not as man seeth; for **man looketh on the outward** appearance, but **the LORD looketh on the heart**."*
(1 Samuel 16:7)

"God is no respecter of persons." (Acts 10:34)

CONCERNING GOD'S WORD

*"For the **prophecy came not** in old time **by the will of man**: but holy men of God spake as **they were moved by the Holy Ghost**."* (2 Peter 1:21)

As you can plainly see, **Mormonism differs from Christianity at its very heart**: Who **God** is, **Jesus** and **The Gospel** plan of salvation. It is our prayer that all will see the deception that the devil has perpetrated on many dear souls. That they will turn from trusting in a religion and their works and trust in the finished work of the Lord Jesus Christ for the salvation of their souls.

"He that rejecteth me, and receiveth not my words, hath one that judgeth him: the word that I have spoken, the same shall judge him in the last day." (John 12:48)

REFERENCES

1 Doctrine and Covenants 1:30 and Mormon Doctrine by Bruce R. McConkie, p. 136

2 Mormon Doctrine by Bruce R. McConkie, pp. 613, 844; Journal of Discourses, Vol. 3, p. 93 and Teachings of the Prophet Joseph Smith by Joseph Fielding Smith, p. 346

3 Mormon Doctrine by Bruce R. McConkie, p. 224

4 Pearl of Great Price, Abraham 3:2-3 and Mormon Doctrine by Bruce R. McConkie, p. 428

5 Teachings of the Prophet Joseph Smith by Joseph Fielding Smith, p. 345 and Gospel Through the Ages by Milton R. Hunter, pp. 104, 114-115

6 The Seer by Orson Pratt, p. 132

7 The Seer by Orson Pratt, p. 172 and Brigham Young and His Wives by John J. Stewart, p. 41

8 Gospel Through the Ages by Milton R. Hunter, p. 127 and Mormon Doctrine by Bruce R. McConkie, pp. 589, 750-751

9 Gospel Through the Ages by Milton R. Hunter, pp. 15, 21 and Mormon Doctrine by Bruce R. McConkie, pp. 192-193, 590

10 Pearl of Great Price, Moses 4:1

11 Mormon Doctrine by Bruce R. McConkie, pp. 193, 618

12 The Contributor, Vol. 6, pp. 296-297 and Race Problems — As They Affect The Church, Address by Mark E. Peterson, August 27, 1954 and Mormon Doctrine by Bruce R. McConkie, 1966, p. 527

13 Journal of Discourses, Vol. 1, p. 63

14 LDS 4th Article of Faith and Mormon Doctrine by Bruce R. McConkie, p. 70

15 Articles of Faith by Talmage, pp. 205-206; and Mormon Doctrine by Bruce R. McConkie, p. 595

16 Pearl of Great Price, Joseph Smith History 1:1-20

17 Pearl of Great Price, Joseph Smith History 1:30-35 and Our Heritage, p. 7

18 Our Heritage, published by the LDS church, p. 4

19 See the 1833 edition of the Book of Commandments (now known as the Doctrine and Covenants) the 1835 edition of the Doctrine and Covenants and Doctrine and Covenants 115:4

20 Doctrines of Salvation by Joseph Fielding Smith, Vol. 1, p. 134-135; History of the Church, Vol. 5, p. 296; Journal of Discourses, Vol. 4, pp. 49-51, 53-54

21 Lorenzo Snow, Millennial Star, Vol. 54, p. 404

22 History of the Church, Vol. 6, pp. 432, 448

23 Doctrine and Covenants 135:4

24 Ward Teachers Lesson for Jan. 1922

25 History of the Church, Vol. 6, pp. 617-618 and Vol. 7, pp. 102-103

26 Mormon Doctrine by Bruce R. McConkie, p. 670

27 LDS 8th Article of Faith

28 Trumpeter of God by Ivan J. Barrett

29 Doctrine and Covenants 132 ~ Official Declaration–1, Mormon Doctrine by Bruce R. McConkie, 1966, p. 527 ~ Official Declaration–2 and Journal of Discourses, Vol. 1, p. 50 ~ Church News, Oct. 9, 1976

30 Official Declaration–1

31 Journal of Discourses, Vol. 11, p. 269

32 Doctrine and Covenants 132:4, 6

33 Mormon Doctrine by Bruce R. McConkie, pp. 116-118

34 Journal of Discourses, Vol. 5, p. 291

35 History of the Church, Vol. 4, p. 461

36 Joseph Smith – Seeker After Truth, pp. 177-178

37 The Seer by Orson Pratt, p. 37-39 and Brigham Young and His Wives by John J. Stewart, p. 41

38 Book of Mormon, Moroni 10:4

39 Mormon Doctrine by Bruce R. McConkie, p. 73

40 Mormon Doctrine by Bruce R. McConkie, p. 845

41 Doctrines of Salvation by Joseph Fielding Smith, Vol. 2, pp. 146, 149

42 Mormon Doctrine by Bruce R. McConkie, pp. 641, 669

43 Mormon Doctrine by Bruce R. McConkie, pp. 117-118, 146

44 Journal of Discourses, Vol. 8, p. 115; Doctrines of Salvation by Joseph Fielding Smith, Vol. 1, p. 18; and The Gospel Through the Ages by Milton R. Hunter, p. 120

45 The First Vision Quilt by Colleen Ralson

46 History of the Church, Vol. 2, p. 182; Oliver B. Huntington Journal, book 14; Doctrine and Covenants 84:1-5 and An Address To All Believers In Christ by David Whitmer, pp. 30-31

47 3913 Changes in the Book of Mormon by Jerald and Sandra Tanner

48 Doctrine and Covenants 132:4 and Journal of Discourses, Vol. 20, pp. 28

49 Journal of Discourses, Vol. 1, pp. 50-51 and Vol. 13, p. 95

50 Church News, October 9, 1976

51 The Way to Perfection by Joseph Fielding Smith, pp. 101-102

52 Mormon Doctrine by Bruce R. McConkie, 1966, p. 527

53 Confessions of John D. Lee, 1880, pp. 282-283

54 What's Going On In There? by Chuck Sackett

55 Journal of Discourses, Vol. 6, p. 5

56 History of the Church, Vol. 6, pp. 408-409

57 Book of Commandments 7:3 (now known as the Doctrine and Covenants) and An Address To All Believers In Christ by David Whitmer, p. 12

58 Book of Mormon, 1 Nephi 13:26

59 Doctrine and Covenants 82:7 and Miracle of Forgiveness by Spencer W. Kimball, p. 170

60 Sterling W. Sill, Deseret News, Church Section, p. 7, July 31, 1965; Answers to Gospel Questions by Joseph Fielding Smith, p. 60 and Doctrines of Salvation by Joseph Fielding Smith, Vol. 1, pp. 114-115

61 Pearl of Great Price, Joseph Smith History 1:19

62 Mormon Doctrine by Bruce R. McConkie, pp. 136-137 and Our Heritage, published by the Mormon church, p. 4

ABOUT THIS BOOK

This book is about a sixth generation Mormon's struggle from pain to peace. She tells of her struggle for happiness and peace. A gripping, true story, which everyone should read. It will touch your heart.

Can a Person Know for Sure

...that he is going **directly** TO HEAVEN WHEN HE DIES? Do you mean, "Take one breath on earth and the next one in the presence of God in heaven?"

I am sure that if a person could really know **for sure** – you would want to know, wouldn't you? You would want your little children who trust and look up to you... to know... or your mother or grandmother who is getting older.

Here is a story of a sixth generation Mormon, a young lady who chronicles her struggle with this very question,

... Can I Know?

You will sense her happiness and pride in her early life of religion. You will sense her pain as she struggles to obtain peace with God.

This book is presented by a Bible believing church and a pastor who loves people. We present this book because we owe you the truth and want you to know the **difference between religion and real peace with God.**